ITALIAN

Phrasebook for Kids

AA

About this book

Jane Wightwick
had the idea

Wina Gunn
wrote the pages

Leila & Zeinah Gaafar
(aged 10 and 12) drew the
first pictures in
each chapter

Robert Bowers
(aged 52) drew the other
pictures, and designed
the book

Marc Vitale

did the Italian stuff

Important things that must be included

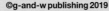

©g-and-w publishing 2019

A CIP catalogue record for this book is available from the British Library

ISBN 978-0-7495-8170-1

Published by AA Media Limited, whose registered office is Grove House, Lutyens Close, Basingstoke, Hampshire RG24 8AG; registered number 06112600.

Printed in UK by MRC Print Ltd.

A05742

What's inside

Making friends

How to be cool with the group

 6

Wanna play?

Our guide to joining in everything from hide-and-seek to the latest electronic game

 30

Feeling hungry

Order your favourite foods or go local

 52

Looking good

Make sure you keep up with all those essential fashions

 62

Hanging out

At the pool, beach, or theme park – don't miss out on the action

70

Pocket money

Spend it here!

90

Grown-up talk

blah! blah! blah! blah!

If you really, really have to!

100

Extra stuff

All the handy things – numbers, months, time, days of the week

108

my big brother il mio fratello grande

👄 eel meeyo fratel-loh granday

grandpa
nonno

👄 non-noh

grandma
nonna

👄 non-nah

ad
apà

👄 pa-pah

mum mamma

👄 mam-mah

my little sister
la mia sorellina

👄 la meeya
sorel-leenah

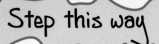

Step this way

stepfather/stepmother
patrigno/matrigna
💋 patreenio/matreenia

stepson/stepdaughter
figliastro/figliastra
💋 feelyeeastroh/
feelyeeastrah

stepbrother/stepsister
fratellastro/sorellastra
💋 fratel-lastroh/
sorel-lastrah

Hi!
Ciao!
💋 chee-ow

What's your name?
Come ti chiami?
💋 komay tee kee-amee

My name's ...
Mi chiamo ...
💋 mee kee-amoh

The word **ciao** means "hello" <u>and</u> "goodbye" – it's such a famous word you might already use it with your English friends. You can say **Ciao, come va?** (*chee-ow, komay vah*, "Hi, how's it going?") or **Ciao, ci vediamo!** (*chee-ow, chee vaydee-amoh*, "Bye, see you later!")

from Canada
dal Canada
🗣 dal kana-da

from Ireland
dall'Irlanda
🗣 dal-leerlanda

from Scotland
dalla Scozia
🗣 dal-la skotseea

from Wales
dal Galles
🗣 dal gal-les

from the United States
dagli Stati Uniti
🗣 dalyee statee uneetee

from England
dall'Inghilterra
🗣 dal-lingilter-ra

10

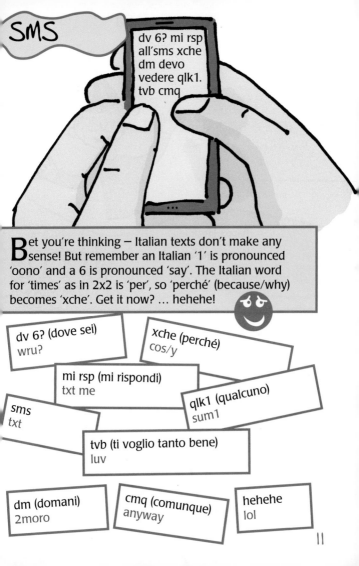

SMS

dv 6? mi rsp all'sms xche dm devo vedere qlk1. tvb cmq

Bet you're thinking – Italian texts don't make any sense! But remember an Italian '1' is pronounced 'oono' and a 6 is pronounced 'say'. The Italian word for 'times' as in 2x2 is 'per', so 'perché' (because/why) becomes 'xche'. Get it now? … hehehe!

dv 6? (dove sei)
wru?

xche (perché)
cos/y

mi rsp (mi rispondi)
txt me

qlk1 (qualcuno)
sum1

sms
txt

tvb (ti voglio tanto bene)
luv

dm (domani)
2moro

cmq (comunque)
anyway

hehehe
lol

How old are you?
Quanti anni hai?
👄 kwantee an-nee eye

12 years old
Dodici anni
👄 dodeechee an-nee

Happy birthday!
Buon compleanno!
👄 boo-on komplayan-no

What's your star sign?
Di che segno sei?
👄 dee kay sayneeo say

When's your birthday?
Quando è il tuo compleanno?
👄 kwando ay eel too-oh komplayan-no

12

Star signs

AQUARIUS
Jan. 21 – Feb. 19
Acquario 💋 ak-kwaraoh

PISCES
Feb. 20 – Mar. 20
Pesci 💋 payshi

ARIES
Mar. 21 – Apr. 20
Ariete 💋 aree-aytay

TAURUS
Apr. 21 – May. 21
Toro 💋 toroh

GEMINI
May 22 – June 21
Gemelli 💋 jaymel-lee

CANCER
June 22 – July 23
Cancro 💋 kankroh

LEO
July 24 – Aug. 23
Leone 💋 layonay

VIRGO
Aug. 24 – Sep. 23
Vergine 💋 vayrjeenay

LIBRA
Sep. 24 – Oct. 23
Bilancia 💋 beelancheea

SCORPIO
Oct. 24 – Nov. 22
Scorpione 💋 skorpeeonay

SAGITTARIUS
Nov. 23 – Dec. 21
Sagittario 💋 sajeet-tareeo

CAPRICORN
Dec. 22 – Jan. 20
Capricorno 💋 kapreecorno

13

14

football il calcio
👄 kalchee-oh

rollerblading
il pattinaggio
👄 pat-teenaj-jeeoh

music
la musica
👄 moozikah

electronic games
i giochi elettronici
👄 ee jee-okee aylet-tr-roneechee

tv
la tele
👄 la taylay

comics
i fumetti
👄 ee foomayt-tee

school la scuola
👄 la skwolah

spiders i ragni
👄 ee ranyee

15

What's ...?

Qual è ...?

💋 kwalay

your favourite group

il tuo complesso preferito

💋 eel too-oh komples-soh pray-fayreetoh

your favourite colour

il tuo colore preferito

💋 eel too-oh koloray pray-fayreetoh

Page 69

your favourite game

il tuo gioco preferito

💋 eel too-oh jee-okoh pray-fayreetoh

your favourite food
il tuo cibo preferito
🗣 eel too-oh cheeboh
pray-fayreetoh

your favourite ringtone
la tua suoneria preferita
🗣 la too-ah soo-onereeyah
pray-fayreetah

your favourite animal
il tuo animale preferito
🗣 eel too-oh aneemalay
pray-fayreetoh

your favourite team
la tua squadra preferita
🗣 la too-ah
skwadra pray-
fayreetah

Talk about your pets

He's hungry
È affamato
👄 ay afah-maytoh

She's sleeping
Sta dormendo
👄 stah dormendoh

Can I stroke your dog?
Posso accarezzare il tuo cane?
👄 possoh akaraytzaray eel too-oh kanay

Do you have
any pets?
Hai qualche animali?
👄 eye kwalkay aneemah-lee

18

dog
cane

🗣 eel kanay

cat
il gatto

🗣 eel gat-toh

snake
il serpente

🗣 eel sairpayntay

guinea pig
il porcellino d'India

🗣 eel porchel-leenoh
deendeea

hamster
il criceto

🗣 eel crichaytoh

budgie
il pappagallino

🗣 eel pap-
pagal-leenoh

My Little doggy goes *"bau bau"*!

An Italian doggy doesn't say "woof, woof", it says *bau, bau* (*baoo, baoo*). An Italian bird says *pio, pio* (*pee-o, pee-o*) and a "cock-a-doodle-do" in Italian chicken-speak is *chicchirichì* (*keek-kee ree-kee*). But a cat does say "miao" and a cow "moo" whether they're speaking Italian or English!

19

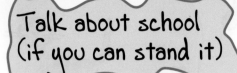

Talk about school (if you can stand it)

geography
la geografia
 lah jayografeea

PE
l'educazione fisica
 laydooka-
tseeonay feezeekah

art
l'educazione artistica
laydooka–tseeonay
arteesteekah

 Italian
m.smith
form 2b

Italian
l'italiano
leetaleeano

maths
la matematica
 la matay–mateekah

20

music
la musica
🗣 la moozeekah

English
l'inglese
🗣 leenglayzay

history
la storia
🗣 la storeeah

science
le scienze
🗣 lay shee-enzay

21

IT

il computer

👄 eel "computer"

Way unfair!

Italian children hardly ever have to wear uniform to school nowadays (but in primary school they used to wear overalls, white with a big blue bow for girls and blue with a big white bow for boys!). Summer holidays are very long, sometimes even up to 12 weeks. But before you turn green with envy, you might not like the dreaded **ripetizioni** (*reepay-teetsee-onee*) or "vacation classes", which you have to take if you fail your end-of-year exams. And if your marks are really bad the teachers could make you repeat the whole year with your little sister!

Talk about your phone

That's ancient
Che vecchio!
👄 kay vekyoh

I've run out of credit
Ho finito i soldi
👄 oh fineetoh ee soldee

What's your mobile like?
Com'è il tuo telefonino?
👄 komay eel too-oh taylayfoneenoh

Lucky!
Sei troppo fortunato!
👄 say troppo fortoon-atoh

What a great ringtone!
Che bella la tua suoneria!
👄 kay bella lah too-ah soo-onereeyah

Gossip

Can you keep a secret?
Sai mantenere un segreto?
👄 sah-ee
mantaynayray
oon saygretoh

Do you have a boyfriend (a girlfriend)?
Ce l'hai il ragazzo (la ragazza)?
👄 chay l'eye
eel ragatsoh
(lah ragatsah)

An OK guy/ An OK girl
Un tipo simpatico/ Una tipa simpatica
👄 oon teepo seempateekoh/
oona teepa seempateekah

What a bossy-boots!
Che prepotente!
👄 kay
praypotayntay

He's nutty/She's nutty!
È uno svitato/È una svitata!
👄 ay oono sveetatoh/
ay oona sveetatah

svitato means 'unscrewed'!

What a misery guts!
Che lagna!
👄 kay laneea

You won't make many friends saying this!

Bog off!
Levati dai piedi!
🗨 layvatee die peeaydee
That means "get off my feet"!

Shut up! **Sta' zitto!**
🗨 stah dzeet–toh

you're fed up with someone, and you want to say
omething like "you silly …!" or "you stupid …!" you can start
with **testa di** … (which actually means "head of …") and add
nything you like. The most common are:

Cabbage head!
Testa di cavolo!
taystah dee kavoloh

Turnip head!
Testa di rapa!
taystah dee rapah

ake your pick. You could also start with **pezzo di** …
piece of …") and say **pezzo d'idiota!** (*paytso deedee-otah*).
ou don't need a translation here, do you?

25

You might have to say

Bother!
Uffa!
👄 oof-fah

Rats!
Mannaggia!
👄 man-naj-jeeah

That's not funny
Non fa ridere nessuno
👄 non fah reedayray nesoonoh

I'm fed up
Sono stufo! (boys)
Sono stufa! (girls)
👄 sono stoofoh
   sono stoofah

That's plenty!
Basta così!
👄 bastah kozee

Stop it!
Smettila!
 smayt—teela

I want to go home!
Voglio tornare a casa!
 volyoh tornaray ah kaza

I don't care
Non me ne importa niente
 non may nay importah neeayntay

At last!
Finalmente!
 feenalmayntay

Saying goodbye

What's your address?

Qual è il tuo indirizzo?

👄 kwalay eel too-oh eendeereetso

Here's my address

Ecco il mio indirizzo

👄 ekko eel meeo eendeereetso

Come to visit me

Vieni a trovarmi

👄 vee-aynee ah trovarmee

Have a good trip!

Buon viaggio!

👄 bwon veeajeeoh

Write to me soon

Scrivimi presto

👄 skreeveemee praystoh

Send me a text

Mandami un messaggio

👄 mandamee oon messah–jeeyo

Do you like chatting online?

Hai voglia di chattare?

👄 eye volyah dee chattaray

Bye!

Ciao!

👄 chee-ow

What's your email address?

Qual è la tua mail?

👄 kwalay la too-ah mail

ↄ□@Ʒ◇*@ᴎ.com

29

WANNA PLAY?

l'elastico

🗣 laylasteeko

il ping-pong

🗣 eel peeng-pong

MP3 player
il lettore
 eel laytoray

il telefonino
 eel taylayfoneenoh

lo yo-yo
 loh "yo-yo"

WANNA PLAY?

Do you want to play ...?

Vuoi giocare ...?

👄 voo-oi jokaray

... table football?

... a calcetto?

👄 ah kal-chayt-toh

... cards?

... a carte?

👄 ah kartay

... on the computer?

... al computer?

👄 al komputer

... hangman?

... all'impiccato?

👄 al-leempeek-katoh

Fancy a game of **leap the foal** or **pretty statues**?

In Italy, tag is called **chiapparello** (*kiap-parel-loh*), which sort of means "catchy-poos"! And instead of leap frog, Italian children play leap "foal" – **la cavallina** (*lah caval-leenah*). Another very popular game is **belle statuine** (*bellay statoo-eenay*) or "pretty statues", which is similar to "big bad wolf". When someone is standing around doing nothing, Italians will often ask "Are you playing pretty statues?" – **Fai la bella statuina?** (*fie lah bellah statoo-eenah*).

Can my friend play too?
Può giocare anche il mio amico?

💋 poo-o jeeokaray ankay eel mee-yo ameekoh?

I have to ask my parents
Devo chiedere ai miei genitori

💋 dayvoh keeaydayray eye mee-ay jayneetoree

Make yourself heard

Who dares?

You're it!
Stai sotto tu!
👄 sty sot-to too

Race you!
Facciamo una corsa?
👄 facheeamoh oona korsah

I'm first
Sono primo io (boy)
Sono prima io (girl)
👄 sonoh preemoh eeo
sonoh preemah eeo

Electronic games

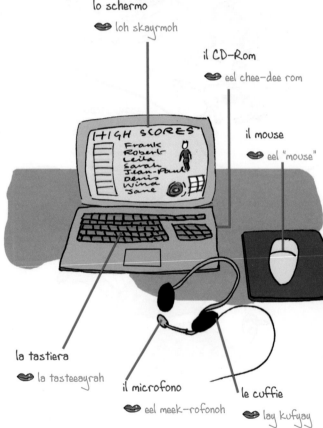

lo schermo
🗣 loh skayrmoh

il CD-Rom
🗣 eel chee-dee rom

il mouse
🗣 eel "mouse"

la tastiera
🗣 la tasteeayrah

il microfono
🗣 eel meek-rofonoh

le cuffie
🗣 lay kufyay

38

Show me
Fammi vedere
 fam-mee vaydayray

What do I do?
Che devo fare?
👄 kay dayvoh faray

Am I dead?
Sono morto?
👄 sonoh
mortoh

Shoot-em-up!
Spara!
👄 sparah

How many lives do I have?
Quante vite ho?
👄 kwantay veetay oh

How many levels are there?
Quanti livelli ci sono?
👄 kwantee leevayl-lee chee sonoh

It's virtual fun!

Do you have WiFi?
Hai WiFi?

 eye "weefee"

Make sure you say it like this to avoid blank looks!

Send me a message.
Mandami un messaggio.

How do i join?
Come m'iscrivo?

I'm not old enough.
Non sono grande abbastanza.

I'm not allowed.
Non mi è permesso.

I don't know who you are.
Non so chi sei.

my blog
il mio blog
🗩 eel meeyo
"blog"

my friends
i miei amici
🗩 ee mee–ay ameechee

my photos
le mie foto
🗩 lay mee–ay fotoh

y videos
miei video
🗩 ee mee–ay vee–dayoh

y music la mia musica
🗩 la meeyah moosikah

41

Non couch-potato activities!

tennis

il tennis

👄 eel ten-nees

trampolining

il trampolino

👄 eel trampoleenoh

bowling

il bowling

👄 eel boolee[n]

swimming

il nuoto

👄 eel noo-oto

42

hockey
l'hockey
👄 lok-kay

gymnastics
la ginnastica
👄 la jeen-nasteekah

ballet
la danza classica
👄 la dantsa klas-seekah

basketball
la pallacanestro
👄 la pal-lakanaystroh

and, of course, we haven't forgotten *"il calcio"*… (P.T.O.) 43

football

boots

gli scarponcini

👄 lyee skarponcheenee

football kit

la divisa da calcio

👄 lah deeveezah dah kalche

ref

l'arbitro

👄 larbeetroh

shin pads

i parastinchi

👄 ee parasteenkee

Good save!

Ben parato!

👄 ben paratoh

Pass! Passa!

👄 pas-sah

44

Offside!
Fuori gioco!
🗣 foo-oree jeeoko

Hands!
Fallo di mano!
🗣 fal-lo dee mano

You're in my team
Tu sei con noi
🗣 too say kon noy

crossbar
la traversa
🗣 la travayrsah

goalpost
il palo
🗣 eel palo

goal
la porta
🗣 la portah

goalie
il portiere
🗣 eel porteeayray

45

Keeping the others in line

Not like that!

Così no!

 kozee noh

You cheat! Sei un imbroglione! (boys only)

Sei un'imbrogliona! (girls only)

 say oon eembrolyee-onay

say oon eembrolyee-onah

I'm not playing anymore

Non gioco più

non jeeoko

peeoo

It's not fair!

Non vale!

non valay

Stop it!

Smettila!

smayt-teela

47

Showing off

... do a handstand?
... fare la verticale?
👄 faray la vayrteecalay

Can you ...
Sai ...
👄 sah-ee

Look at me!
Guardatemi!
👄 gooardataymee

... do a cartwheel?
... fare la ruota?
👄 ... fare la ruota?

... do this?
... fare questo?
👄 faray kwaystoh

48

Tongue tied

Impress your Italian friends with this!

Show off to your new Italian friends by practising this **scioglilingua** (*shee-olyeleen-gooa*), or tongue twister:

Sopra la panca la capra campa, sotto la panca la capra crepa.

soprah la pankah la kaprah kampah, sot-toh la pankah la kaprah kraypah

This means "On the bench the goat lives, under the bench the goat dies.")

Then see if they can do as well with this English one:

"She sells seashells on the seashore, but the shells she sells aren't seashells, I'm sure."

49

For a rainy day

pack of cards
mazzo di carte
👄 matso dee kartay

my deal/your deal
do io le carte/dai tu le carte
👄 dahray eo lay kartay/ die too lay kartay

king
il re
👄 eel ray

queen
la regina
👄 la rayjeenah

jack
il fante
👄 eel fantay

joker
il jolly
👄 eel jol-lee

fiori
👄 feeoree

cuori
👄 koo-oree

picche
👄 peek-kay

quadri
👄 kwadree

Do you have the ace of swords?!

You may see Italian children playing with different playing cards. There are only 40 cards instead of 52 and the suits are different. Instead of clubs, spades, diamonds and hearts, there are gold coins (**denari** *daynaree*), swords (**spade** *spahday*), cups (**coppe** *koppay*) and sticks (**bastoni** *bastonee*).

chessboard la scacchiera 👄 la skak-keeayrah

bishop l'alfiere 👄 lalfeeayray

knight il cavallo 👄 eel kaval-loh

rook la torre 👄 lah torray

queen la regina 👄 lah rayjeeanah

awn

pedone 👄 eel paydonay

.ing il re 👄 eel ray

51

FEELING HUNGRY

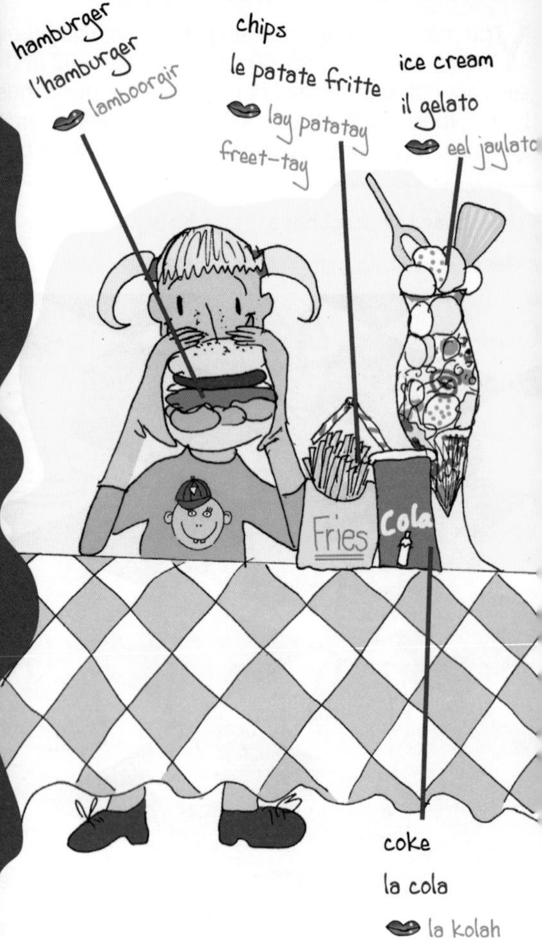

squid
i calamari
ee kalamaree

creme caramel
il crème caramel
eel krem karamel

mussels
le cozze
lay kotsay

orange juice
il succo d'arancia
eel sook-koh
darancheeah

FEELING HUNGRY

Grub

I'm starving

Ho una fame da lupo

💋 oh oona famay dah loopoh

il lupo

That means "I have the hunger of a wolf"!

Please can I have ...

Mi dà ...

💋 mee dah

... a croissant

... un cornetto

🗣 oon cornayt-toh

... a chocolate bun

... un pasticcino al cioccolato

🗣 oon pasteech-cheeno al chok-kolatoh

... a sandwich

... un tramezzino

🗣 oon tramay-dzeeno

... a slice of pizza

... un pezzo di pizza

🗣 oon paytso dee peetsa

... folded pizza

... un calzone

🗣 oon caltsonay

In the winter, you can buy bags of delicious roasted chestnuts from street sellers, hot and ready to eat!

... a bag of chestnuts

un cartoccio di castagne

👄 oon kartocheeo dee kastaneeay

Take-away pizza in Italy is often sold **al taglio** (*al talyee-oh*), which means it is cut into rectangular slices from a large baking sheet … and you can buy as big a piece as you like. Another great midday snack is a **calzone** (*caltsonay*), which is a round pizza folded in half to look like a pastie, with all the juicy bits inside.

Drink up

I'm dying for
a drink
Muoio di sete
👄 moo-oyo dee
saytay

I'd like ...
Vorrei ...
👄 vor-ray

... a coke
... una cola
👄 oona kolah

... an orange juice
... un succo d'arancia
👄 oon sook-koh darancheeah

... an apple juice
... un succo di mela
👄 oon sook-koh dee mayla

If you want something really cold and slushy in the summer you can ask for **una granita** (*oona graneetah*), which is crushed ice with fruit juice or squash.

water

acqua

 akkwah

... a squash

... uno sciroppo

👄 oonoh sheerop-poh

... a milkshake

... un frullato

👄 oon frool-latoh

If you're really lucky you might go to Italy during **Carnevale** in February. Adults and kids dress up in the weirdest costumes and everyone goes loopy for a few days. There are lots of special sticky cakes like **frappe** (*frappay*): big pastry bows dipped in icing sugar; and **castagnole** (*kastanyolay*): delicious fried balls of pastry covered in sugar.

You: Can I have some castagnole, Mum?

Mum: No. They'll make you fat and rot your teeth.

You: But I think it's good to experience a foreign culture through authentic local food.

Mum: Oh, all right then.

That's lovely
È buonissimo
👄 ay boo-onees-seemoh

How did you like it?

That's gorgeous
È squisito
👄 ay skweezeetoh

I don't like that
Non mi piace
👄 non mee pee-achay

I'm stuffed
Sono pieno (boys)
Sono piena (girls)
👄 sonoh peeaynoh
sonoh peeaynah

can't eat that
esto non lo posso mangiare
👄 kwaysto non lo pos-soh
njeearay

That's gross
Che schifo
👄 kay skeefoh

59

Pasta Pasta Pasta!

Italians, especially those from Naples, claim to have invented pasta. There are lots of different types of pasta and just as many, if not more, different sauces to go with them, including a sauce made with squid ink! You have probably heard of **spaghetti** and **tagliatelle**, but what about these:

penne (quills)

farfalle (butterflies)

lumache (snails!)

ruote (wheels)

stelline (little stars)

Parties

balloon il palloncino
🗨 eel paloncheeno

Can I have some more?
Potrei averne un altro po'?
🗨 potray avairnay oon altroh po

party hat
il cappello da festa
🗨 eel kap-pello dah festa

This is for you
Questo è per te
🗨 kwaysto ay payr tay

What do Italian children play at birthday parties?

Pasta parcel!

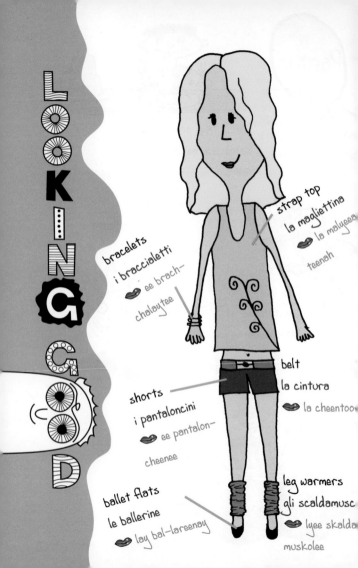

LOOKING GOOD

strap top
la magliettina
🗣 la malyeea-
teenah

bracelets
i braccialetti
🗣 ee brach-
chalaytee

belt
la cintura
🗣 la cheentoo-

shorts
i pantaloncini
🗣 ee pantalon-
cheenee

ballet flats
le ballerine
🗣 lay bal-lareenay

leg warmers
gli scaldamusc
🗣 lyee skalda-
muskolee

cap
il berretto
🫘 eel ber-rayt-toh

earphones
gli auricolari
🫘 ee owree-
koolar-ree

sweatshirt
la felpa
🫘 la faylpah

jeans
i jeans
🫘 ee jeens

trainers
gli scarponcini
🫘 lyee skarponcheenee

LOOKING GOOD

Clothes

jeans
i jeans
👄 ee jeens

sweatshirt
la felpa
👄 la faylp

T-shirt
la maglietta
👄 lah malyeeayt-t

football shirt
la maglietta da calcio
👄 lah malyeeayt-tah da calcheeo

trainers
gli scarponcini
👄 lyee skarponcheenee

skirt

la gonna

 la gon-nah

dress

il vestito

eel vaysteetoh

trousers

i pantaloni

ee pantalonee

shorts

i pantaloncini

ee pantaloncheenee

shoes

scarpe

lay skarpay

That T-shirt, please
Quella maglietta per favore
🗨 kwel-lah malyeeayt-
tah payr favoray

Cool tattoo!
Che bel tatuaggio!
🗨 kay bel tatooaj-jeeoh

The pink frilly one
Quella rosa con i fronzoli
🗨 kwel-lah rozah kon ee
frondzolee

The purple stripey one
Quella viola a strisce
🗨 kwayl-lah veeola
ah streeshay

Awesome miniskirt!
Che minigonna fantastica!
🗨 kay meeneegon-nah
fantasteekah

She's got an orange hair!
There are lots of double letters in
Italian. Saying the double letter
properly can be very important.
For example, a hat is **un cappello**
(*oon cap-payl-loh*), with two "p"s,
but a hair is **un capello** (*oon
capayl-lo*).

66

spotty
a pois

👄 ah pooah

flowery
a fiori

👄 ah feeoree

frilly
con i fronzoli

👄 kon ee frondzolee

glittery
luccicante

👄 luch-cheekantay

stripey
a strisce

👄 ah streeshay

Make it up!

lip gloss
il lucidalabbra
🗣 eel loocheedah-labrah

glitter gel
il gel luccicante
🗣 eel "gel" luch-cheekantay

I need a mirror
Mi serve uno specchio
🗣 mee servay oono spek-kyo

nail varnish
lo smalto per le unghie
🗣 lo smalto payr lay ungyay

earrings
gli orecchini
🗣 lyee oraykeenee

eye shadow
l'ombretto
🗣 lombrayt-to

Can I borrow your straighteners?
Me lo presti il tuo lisciacapelli?
🗣 may lo prestee eel too-oh leesheeya-kapayllee

68

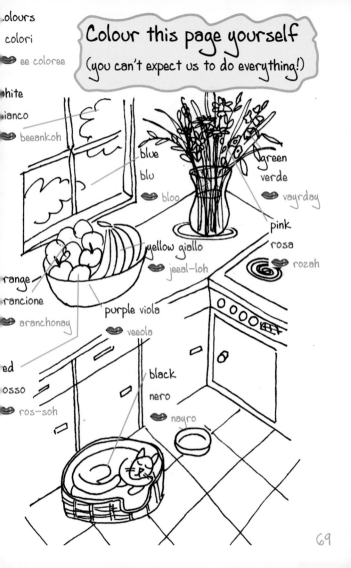

colours
colori
🗣 ee coloree

Colour this page yourself
(you can't expect us to do everything!)

white
bianco
🗣 beeankoh

blue
blu
🗣 bloo

green
verde
🗣 vayrday

pink
rosa
🗣 rozah

yellow giallo
🗣 jeeal-loh

orange
arancione
🗣 aranchonay

purple viola
🗣 veeola

red
rosso
🗣 ros-soh

black
nero
🗣 nayro

69

What should we do?

Che facciamo?

🗨 kay facheeamoh

Can I come too?

Vengo anch'io?

🗨 vayngo ankeeoh

Where do you lot hang out?

Dove v'incontrate?

🗨 dovay veenkontratay

That's really wicked

Che forte

🗨 kay fortay

I'm not allowed

Non mi lasciano

🗨 non mee lasheeanoh

Let's go back Torniamo indietro

🗣 torneeamoh indeeaytroh

That gives me goose bumps (or "goose flesh" in Italian!)
Mi fa venire la pelle d'oca

🗣 mee fah vayneeray la payl-lay dokah

I'm bored to death
Sto morendo dalla noia

🗣 stoh morayndoh dal-la noya

HOUSE OF MIRRORS

That's a laugh
Quello è buffissimo

🗣 kwel-lo ay boof-fees-seemoh

Beach babes

Can I borrow this?

Me lo presti?

👄 may loh praystee

Let's hit the beach

Tutti al mare

👄 toot-tee al marau

Is this your bucket?

È tuo questo secchiello?

👄 ay too-o kwestoh saykeeayl-lo

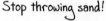

You can bury me

Mi puoi seppellire

👄 mee poo-oee sayp-payl-leeray

Stop throwing sand!

Smetti di tirare la sabbia!

👄 smayt-tee dee teeraray la sab-beeah

Mind my eyes!

Non mi buttare la sabbia negli occhi!

👄 non mee boot-taray la sab-beea nelyee ok-kee

74

andcastle
castello di sabbia
eel kastayl-loh dee ab-beeah

sea
il mare
eel maray

beach
la spiaggia
la speeaj-jah

tōwel
l'asciugamano
lashoogamanoh

swimming costume
il costume da bagno
eel kostoomay dah banyeeoh

bucket il secchiello
eel sayk-keeayl-loh

snorkel
boccaglio
eel bok-kaleeyo

shells
le conchiglie
lay konkeelyeeay

spade
la paletta
la palayt-tah

75

It's going swimmingly!

How to make a splash in Italian!

Let's hit the swimming pool

Tutti in piscina

🗨 toot-tee een peesheena

Can you swim (underwater)?

Sai nuotare (sott'acqua)?

🗨 saee nwotaray (sot-takwa)

Me too/I can't

Anch'io/Io no

🗨 ankeeo/eeo noh

Can you dive?

Ti sai tuffare?

🗨 tee sah-ee toof-faray

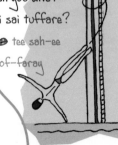

I'm getting changed

Mi sto cambiando

🗨 mee stoh kambeeandoh

... backstroke

il dorso

 eel dorsoh

Can you do ...?

Sai fare ...?

sah-ee faray

... butterfly

la farfalla

la farfal-la

... crawl

il stile libero

eel steelay leebayroh

breaststroke

la rana la ranah

[which means "the frog", and, let's face it, that's what you look like!]

slide

lo scivolo

loh sheevoloh

goggles gli occhialini

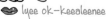
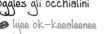
 lyee ok-keealeenee

Downtown

Do you know the way?
Sai la strada?

💋 sah-ee la stradah

Italy has a high-speed train called the **Pendolino**, which means 'leaning over', because the carriages lean to the side when it speeds round bends. Persuade your parents to try it – it's better than a roller-coaster at the fun fair!

Let's ask
Chiediamo

💋 kyee-aydeeamoh

bus
l'autobus

💋 laootoboos

Is it far?

È lontano?

👄 ay lontanoh

Are we allowed in here?

Possiamo entrare?

👄 pos–seeamoh ayntraray

car

la macchina

👄 lah mak–keenah

The "proper" Italian word for car is **automobile** (*aooto-mobeelay*) but you'll look much cooler if you say **macchina** (*mak-keenah*) or, if the car has seen better days, **macinino** (*macheeneenoh*). Use the cooler short words instead of those long untrendy ones the adults will try and make you say: **bici** (*beechee*) instead of **bicicletta**, **moto** instead of **motocicletta** and **bus** (*boos*) instead of **autobus**.

79

Park yourself here

swings le altalene
— lay altalaynay

climbing frame il quadro
svedese — eel kwadro
zvedaysay

playground il parco giochi
— eel parko jeeokee

grass il prato
— eel prato

tree l'albero
— lalbayro

slide
lo scivolo
— lo sheevolo

park il parco — eel parko

Can we play ball games?

Giochiamo a palla?

 jeeokee-ahmo a palla

roundabout

la giostra

 la gee-ostra

sandpit

la sabbia

la sab-beeya

Can I have a go? Mi fai provare?

mee faee provaray

Picnics

I hate wasps

Odio le vespe

🫦 odeeo lay vayspay

Move over!

Fatti più in là!

🫦 fat-tee

peeoo een lah

bread

il pane 🫦 eel panay

napkin

il tovagliolo

🫦 eel tovalyeeolo

Let's sit here

Sediamoci qui

🫦 saydeeamochee kwee

ham il prosciutto

🫦 eel proshoot-to

cheese

il formaggio

🫦 eel formaj-jeeo

yoghurt

lo yogurt

🫦 loh yogoort

crisps

le patatine

🫦 lay patateenay

drinks
le bibite
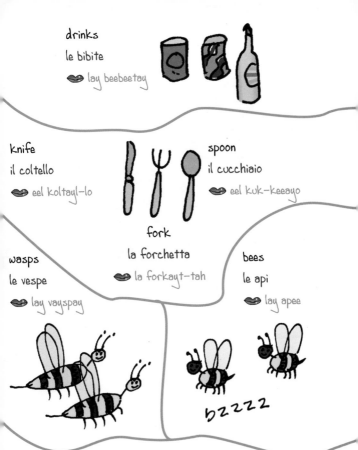 lay beebeetay

knife
il coltello
eel koltayl-lo

spoon
il cucchiaio
eel kuk-keeayo

fork
la forchetta
la forkayt-tah

wasps
le vespe
lay vayspay

bees
le api
lay apee

bzzzz

ants
le formiche
 lay formeekay

Wake up, campers!

tent la tenda
🗨 la taynda

tent peg
il picchetto
🗨 eel peek-kayt-toh

camper van
il camper
🗨 eel "camper"

penknife
il coltellino svizzero
🗨 eel koltayl-leeno zveet-tzayro

stove
il fornello
🗨 eel fornayllo

sleeping bag il sacco a pelo
🗨 eel sakko a paylo

torch la torcia
🗨 la torcheeya

84

That tent's a palace!
Quella tenda è un palazzo!
🗣 kwella taynda ay oon palat-zoh

ampfire
fuoco d'accampamento
🗣 eel foo-oko
akampa-maynto

I've lost my torch
Ho perso la mia torcia
🗣 oh payrso la meeya torcheeya

The showers are gross!
Le docce fanno schifo!
🗣 lay dotchay fanno skeefo

Where does the rubbish go?
Dove va la spazzatura?
🗣 dovay vah la spatza-toorah

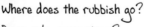

All the fun of the fair

helter-skelter
lo scivolo
👄 loh sheevolo

big wheel la ruota panoramica
👄 la rwotah panorameeka

house of mirrors
la casa degli specchi
👄 la kasah delyee spayk-kee

dodgems
l'autoscontro
👄 laootoskontro

Let's try this
Andiamo su questo
👄 andeeamo soo kwesto

roundabout
la giostra
🔊 la jeeostra

It's (too) fast
Va (troppo) forte
🔊 vah trop-po fortay

That's for babies
Quello è per i bambini
🔊 kwayl-lo ay payr ee ambeenee

Do you get wet here?
Qui ci si bagna?
🔊 kwee chee see banya

I'm not going on my own
Da solo/a non ci vado
🔊 dah solo/a non chee vado

Disco nights

mirror ball
la palla
specchiata
👄 la palla
spayk-kyata

loudspeaker
la cassa
👄 la kas-sa

Can I request a song?
Posso chiedere una canzone?
👄 posso kee-ayderay oona kanzonay

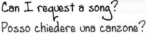

The music is really lame
La musica è troppo noiosa
👄 la mooseeka ay troppo noyosa

spotlight
lo spot
👄 loh "spot"

DJ
il DJ
👄 eel "DJ"

turntable la piatta-
forma girante 👄 la
pyattaforma geeranta

How old do I need to be?
Quanti anni devo avere?
🗨 kwantee annee dayvo averay

dance floor
la pista da ballo
🗨 la peesta dah ballo

Shall we dance?
Balliamo?
🗨 bal-lyahmo

I love this song!
Questa canzone mi
fa impazzire!
🗨 kwaysta
kanzonay mee fah
mpat-zeeray

89

POCKET MONEY

sweets
le caramelle
👄 lay karamayl-lay

T-shirts
le magliette
👄 lay malyeeayt-t

toys
i giocattoli
👄 ee jeeokat-tolee

shop assistant
il commesso
👄 eel kom-mays—

books

i libri

 ee leebree

il mobile

eel "mobile"

pencils

le matite

lay mateetay

P
O
C
K
E
T
M
O
N
E
Y

What does that sign say?

Macelleria

cake shop
pasticceria
👄 pastee-chayreeah

Pasticceria

butcher shop
macelleria
👄 machayl-layreeah

bakery
panetteria
👄 panayt-tayreea

Panetteria

sweet shop
negozio di dolciumi
👄 naygotseeo dee dolcheeoomee

Fruttivendol

stationers
cartoleria
👄 kartolayreeah

Cartoleria

greengrocer
fruttivendolo
👄 froot-teevayndoloh

Negozio di abbigliamento

clothes shop
negozio di abbigliamento
👄 naygotseeo dee ab-beelyeeamaynto

92

Do you have some dosh?

Ce l'hai qualche soldo?

💬 chay lie kwalkay soldo

I'm skint

Sono al verde

💬 sono al vayrday

I'm loaded

Sono ricco sfondato

💬 sono reek-ko sfondato

Here you go

Tieni

💬 teeaynee

This shop is weird!

Questo negozio è strano!

💬 kwesto naygot-seeo ay strah-no

That's a bargain È un affare

💬 ay oon af-faray

It's a rip-off

Questi ti spellano!

💬 kwaystee tee spayl-lanoh

93

Sweet heaven!

I love this shop

Adoro questo negozio

💋 adohro kwesto naygotseeo

Let's get some sweets

Prendiamo delle caramelle

💋 prayndeeamo dayllay karamayl-lay

Let's get some ice cream

Prendiamo un gelato

💋 prayndeeamo oon jaylatoh

lollipops

lecca lecca

💋 lek-kah

lek-kah

[that means "lick-lick"!]

a bar of chocolate

una tavoletta di cioccolata

💋 oona tavolayt-tah dee chok-kolatah

chewing gum

gomma da masticare

💋 gom-mah dah masteekaray

94

If you really want to look Italian (but end up with lots of fillings) try these:

Baci Perugina
(bachee peroo-jeenah)
The most famous Italian chocolate has to be **baci Perugina** (literally "kisses"), nuggets of chocolate and nuts wrapped in silver paper with little romantic messages for that boy or girl you fancy!

carbone di zucchero
(carbonay dee dzook-kayro)!
Sugar coal. On 6th January, the Epiphany, Italian kids get presents, but those who have been naughty get coal! Actually this is black coal-shaped candy – phew!

pecorelle di zucchero
(paykorayl-lay dee dzook-kayro)
Forget the Easter eggs, try some 'little sugar sheep'!

Kinder sorpresa
(kinder sorpraysah)
You probably know these "Kinder Surprise" chocolate eggs with wicked little toys, but did you know they come from Italy?

Other things you could buy
(that won't ruin your teeth!)

What are you getting?
Tu che prendi?
🫦 too kay prayndee

That toy, please
Quel giocattolo, per favore
🫦 kwayl jeeokat-toloh payr favoray

Two postcards, please
Due cartoline, per favore
🫦 dooay kartoleenay payr favoray

This is rubbish
Questa è robaccia
🫦 kwesta ay robach-cha

This is cool
Questo è eccezionale
🫦 kwesto ay echetseeonalay

I'm getting ...
Io prendo ...

🗣️ Io prendo ...

... a pen
... una penna

🗣️ oona pen-nah

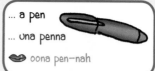

... stamps
... dei francobolli

🗣️ day franko-bol-lee

... felt-tip pens
... dei pennarelli

🗣️ day pen-narel-lee

... coloured pencils
... delle matite colorate

🗣️ dellay mateetay coloratay

... a key ring
... un portachiavi

🗣️ oon portah-kee-avee

... comics
... dei fumetti

🗣️ day foomayt-tee

... a box ... una scatolina

🗣 oona skatoh-leenah

... a fridge magnet

... una calamita da frigorifero

🗣 oona kalameetah dah freego-reefayroh

... a necklace

... una collana

🗣 oona kollana

How much is that?

Quanto costa?

🗣 kwanto kostah

Italian kids, and adults, have always been mad about Disney comics. But did you know that most of the characters have Italian names you wouldn't recognise? Mickey Mouse is **Topolino** ("little mouse"), Goofy is **Pippo**, Donald Duck is **Paperino** ("little duck") and Huey, Dewey and Louie are **Qui, Quo, Qua**!

Money talks

How much pocket money do you get?

Quanta paghetta prendi?

👄 kwantah pagayttah prayndee

I only have this much

Io ho solo questi soldi

👄 eeo oh solo kwestee soldee

Can you lend me
ten euros?

Mi presti dieci euros?

👄 mee praystee
deeaychee yooro

No way!

Neanche per sogno!

👄 nayankay payr
sonyeeo

Italian money is the **euro** (pronounced *ayoo-roh*).
A euro is divided into 100 **centesimi** (*chayntayseemee*).
Coins: 1, 2, 5, 10, 20, 50 **centesimi**
         1, 2 **euros**
Notes: 5, 10, 20, 50, 100 **euros**
Make sure you know how much you are spending
before you blow all your pocket money at once!

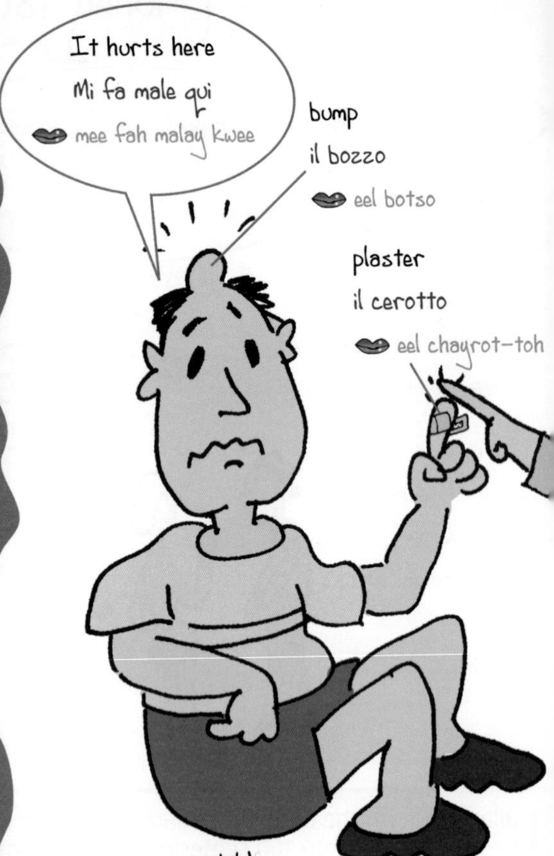

child

bambino/bambina

bambeenoh (boy) / bambeenah (girl)

Help!

Something has broken
Si è rotto qualcosa

 see ay rot-to kwalkozah

Please
Per favore

 payr favoray

Can you help me?
Può aiutarmi?

 pwoh aeeootarmee

Where's the post box?
Dov'è la buca delle lettere?

 dovay lah booka dayl-lay
lay-tayray

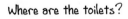

Where are the toilets?
Dov'è il bagno?

  dovay eel banyeeo

I can't manage it

Non ci riesco

💋 non chee ree-aysko

Could you pass me that?

Mi passi quello?

💋 mee pas-see kwayl-lo

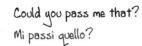

What time is it?

Che ore sono?

💋 kay oray sonoh

Come and see

Vieni a vedere

💋 veeaynee ah vaydayray

May I look at your watch?

Mi fa vedere sul suo orologio

💋 mee fah vaydayray sool
soo-o orolojeeo

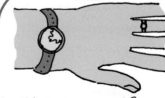

Lost for words

I've lost ...

Ho perso ...

💋 oh payrso

... my ticket

... il mio biglietto

💋 eel meeo bilyee-ayt-to

... my parents

... i miei genitori

💋 ee meeay
jayneetoree

... my mobile

... il mio telefonino

💋 eel meeo
taylayfoneenoh

... my money ... i miei soldi

💬 ee meeay soldee

... my shoes
... le mie scarpe

💬 lay meeay skarpay

... my sweater
... la mia maglia

💬 lah meeah malyeeah

... my watch
... il mio orologio

💬 eel meeoh orolojeeo

... my jacket ... la mia giacca

💬 lah meeah jeeak-kah

105

Adults only!

Show this page to adults who can't seem to make themselves clear (it happens). They will point to a phrase, you read what they mean, and you should all understand each other perfectly.

Non ti preoccupare
Don't worry

Siediti qui
Sit down here

Come ti chiami di nome e di cognome?
What's your name and surname?

Quanti anni hai?
How old are you?

Di dove sei?
Where are you from?

Dove sei alloggiato/a?
Where are you staying?

Cos'è che ti fa male?
Where does it hurt?

Sei allergico/a a qualcosa?
Are you allergic to anything?

È proibito
It's forbidden

Devi essere accompagnato/a da un adulto
You have to have an adult with you

Vado a cercare qualcuno che parli l'inglese
I'll get someone who speaks English

EXTRA STUFF

weather
il tempo
eel taympoh

numbers i numeri ee noomayree

time

l'ora

lorah

EXTRA STUFF

Numbers

Knock, knock.

Who's there?

Uno.

Uno who?

Unos where I got this crummy joke!

1 uno 👄 oonoh

2 due 👄 doo-ay

3 tre 👄 tray

4 quattro 👄 kwat-troh

5 cinque 👄 cheenkway

6 sei 👄 say

110

7 sette
sayt-tay

8 otto
ot-toh

9 nove
novay

10 dieci
deeaychee

11 undici
oondeechee

12 dodici
dodeechee

tredici  traydeechee

quattordici  kwat-tordeechee

quindici kweendeechee

16	sedici	*saydeechee*
17	diciassette	*deechas-set-tay*
18	diciotto	*deechot-toh*
19	diciannove	*dechan-novay*
20	venti	*vayntee*

If you want to say "twenty-two", "sixty-five", and so on, you can just put the two numbers together like you do in English:

| 22 | ventidue | *vaynteedooay* |
| 65 | sessantacinque | *sayss-santacheenkway* |

This works except if you're saying "twenty-one", "sixty-one" and so on. Then you need to remove the final letter from the first number:

| 21 | ventuno (not ventiuno) | *vayntoonoh* |
| 61 | sessantuno
(<u>not</u> sessantauno) | *sayss-santoonoh* |

30	trenta	*trayntah*
40	quaranta	*kwarantah*
50	cinquanta	*cheenkwantah*
60	sessanta	*sayssayntah*
70	settanta	*sayt-tantah*
80	ottanta	*ot-tantah*
90	novanta	*novantah*
100	cento	*chentoh*

a thousand   mille   *meel-lay*

a million   un milione   *oon meel-lyonay*

a gazillion!   un fantastiliardo!   *oon fantasteeylardoh*

You might notice that Italians wave their hands a lot when they speak. What you won't realise is that not all flapping and waving means the same. Try looking out for some of these:

"What do you want?"

"Say that again"

"Are you crazy?"

"He's changed his mind"

March	marzo	*martsoh*
April	aprile	*apreelay*
May	maggio	*madjoh*

June	giugno	*joonyoh*
July	luglio	*loolyoh*
August	agosto	*agostoh*

September	settembre	*set-tembray*
October	ottobre	*ot-tobray*
November	novembre	*novembray*

September	settembre	*set-tembray*
October	ottobre	*ot-tobray*
November	novembre	*novembray*

Seasons

primavera *preemavayrah*

SPRING

estate *estatay*

SUMMER

autunno *owtoon-noh*

AUTUMN

inverno *eenvernoh*

WINTER

118

Days of the week

Monday	lunedì	*loonaydee*
Tuesday	martedì	*martaydee*
Wednesday	mercoledì	*merkolaydee*
Thursday	giovedì	*jovaydee*
Friday	venerdì	*vaynayrdee*
Saturday	sabato	*sabatoh*
Sunday	domenica	*domayneekah*

By the way, school starts at around 8.30 a.m. for most children in Italy and ends around 1.00 p.m., but they also have to go to school on Saturday morning.

Good times

It's ...
Sono ...
👄 sonoh

(five) o'clock
le (cinque)
👄 lay (cheenkway)

quarter past (two)
le (due) e un quarto
👄 lay (dooay) ay oon kwartoh

quarter to (four)
le (quattro) meno un quarto
👄 lay (kwat-troh) maynoh
oon kwartoh

half past (three)
le (tre) e mezzo
👄 lay (tray) ay medzoh

...ve past (ten)

...(dieci) e cinque

🗣 lay (deeaychee) ay cheenkway

twenty past (eleven)

le (undici) e venti

🗣 lay (oondeechee)
ay vayntee

...n to (four)

...(quattro) meno dieci

🗣 lay (kwat-troh) maynoh deeaychee

twenty to (six)

le (sei) meno venti

🗣 lay (say) maynoh vayntee

Watch out for "one o'clock". It's a bit different from the other times. If you want to say "It's one o'clock" you have to say **È l'una** (*ay loonah*). "It's half past one" is **È l'una e mezza** (*ay loonah ay medzah*), and so on.

morning
la mattina

 lah mat-teenah

midday
mezzogiorno

lah medzojorrnoh

afternoon
il pomeriggio

eel pomayreedjoh

evening la sera

lah sayrah

midnight
mezzanotte

medzanot-tay

122

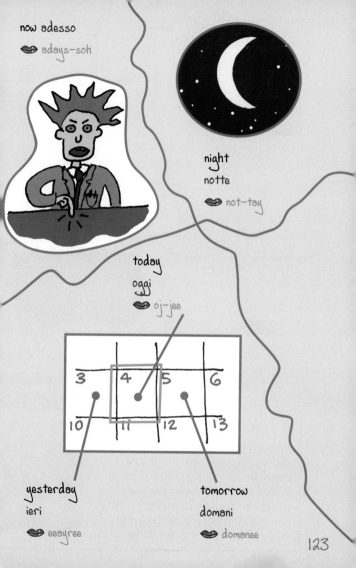

Weather wise

Can we go out?

Possiamo uscire?

👄 pos–seeamoh oosheeray

It's hot

Fa caldo

👄 fah kaldoh

It's cold

Fa freddo

👄 fah frayd–doh

It's a horrible day

Fa cattivo tempo

👄 fa kat–teevoh taympoh

It's raining basins!

When it rains heavily in Italy, people say it's "raining basins": **Piove a catinelle** (*peeovay ah kateenayl-lay*). A well-known saying is **Cielo a pecorelle acqua a catinelle**, or "Small sheep in the sky means basins of water". "Small sheep" are fluffy clouds!

It's windy
C'è vento
👄 chay vayntoh

It's sunny
C'è il sole
👄 chay eel solay

It's raining
Piove
👄 peeovay

It's snowing
Nevica
👄 nayveekah

I'm soaked
Sono fradicio
👄 sono fradeecheeo

It's nice Fa bel tempo
👄 fah bel taympoh

125

Signs of life

Vietato l'uso dei telefonini

Mobile phones not allowed

altezza minima

minimum height

Vietato l'ingress

No Entry

Vietato ai minori di 18 anni

Under 18s not allowed

Vietato ai
maggiori di 5 anni

Over 5s
not allowed